a ONE Chapter Book

The Promise

A story about Personal Success, Heart-Centered Sales and Making an Irresistible Offer

W.T. Hamilton

Award Winning Author of

The Harsh Truths

Copyright © 2020 Your Invincible Power

"When I first connected with WT I knew he was a leader who takes action to make the most out of an opportunity. He knows how to create success and to empower and motivate his clients to do the same. He is an insightful, knowledgeable visionary that gets the job done for his clients."

~ Jim Britt – 13 times bestseller and named as one of the world's top success coaches.

"After 28 years in the speaking industry, when WT and I connected I knew it was a person that saw with vision not sight, that saw a return on investment in one's self. He's gone on to accomplish great things. Learn what he knows. Well deserved!"

~ Jim Lutes – Founder of Lutes International

"WT is a stellar example of tenacity. He is relentless in the pursuit of his passions. He leads with his heart and closes with his head. He's an authentic speaker, dedicated entrepreneur and committed business coach. If you have one person in your corner, make sure it's WT!"

~ Rina Rovinelli – Cofounder of Speaker Slam

~~*

"I've been so fortunate to work with Jim Britt. Can you imagine how amazed and excited I was when I found out that Jim Britt was Tony Robbins' first coach! Jim was also business partners with Jim Rohn!

Then you add the dynamic Jim Lutes, international trainer and mentor to top performers around the world, to the list and you've got a recipe for success.

Learning from these guys helped me really create a life-changing step-by-step, customized action plan that allows my clients to enhance their authenticity, develop mind mastery, create time freedom and build their success on purpose with purpose.

I was also lucky enough to meet and work with Rina Rovinelli and her business partner Dan Shaikh. Rina has been an amazing friend and she has helped me grow leaps and bounds as a speaker. Always giving me honest and helpful constructive feedback.

Since learning and growing with both Jims and Rina I've been lucky enough to learn from Brian Tracy, Sunil Tulsani, Kevin Harrington and the list goes on.

It was by learning the one thing that all these successful people know and that every other successful person knows. It is the one thing that successful people run towards and unsuccessful people run away from.

It's simply this… every successful person has someone that guides them, mentors them and teaches them how to become successful.

That is my mission: to do for you what was done for me."

~ W.T. Hamilton – Author of the One Chapter book series.

All rights reserved

Published by Your Invincible Power Company

No part of this publication may be reproduced, stored in a retrieval system, or transmitted in any form or by any means, electronic, mechanical, photocopied, re-recorded, scanned, or otherwise, except as permitted under Canadian copyright law, without the prior written permission of the author.

Disclaimer:

While the author and publisher of this book has made reasonable effort to ensure the accuracy of the information contained herein, the author and publisher assumes no liability with respect to losses or damage caused, or alleged to be caused, by any reliance on any information contained herein and disclaim any and all warranties, expressed or implied, as to the accuracy or reliability of said information. The author and publisher make no representations or warranties with respect to the accuracy or completeness of the contents of this work and specifically disclaim all warranties. The advice and strategies contained herein may not be suitable for every situation.

Copyright

Your Invincible Power Company(Standard Copyright Licence)

Edition

First Edition

ISBN: 9798638517250
Imprint: Independently published

Published

May 2020

Table of Contents

The Promise 15

Final Thoughts 135

Who is W.T.? 145

Who is George? 151

Big Ups 156

Books by W.T......................................158

From the Cutting Room Floor............164

7 Seconds, 7 Minutes 170

Ya'll think it's boujee, I'm like it's fine but I'm trying to give you a million dollars' worth of game for $9.99

Jay-Z - The Story of O.J.

Chapter 2.32: The Promise

"I want you to make a promise to me right now. Before I really get started I need you to make this promise; it's not really for me, it's completely for you. This is the most important promise you will make to yourself today, possibly this week, or even this year; maybe it will be the most important promise you've ever made to yourself. Are you ready to hear what the promise is?"

George was completely captivated by this statement. He was excitedly and actively listening to what would be said next. And he was not alone. The room was full of engaged listeners all waiting to hear what the speaker was about to ask them.

Everyone had been drawn to this event on an early Saturday morning for one reason: to learn how to create a thriving online business. Driven entrepreneurs from many cities had traveled here to listen to the words of this speaker. Many had been following him for years but for George it was his first time; he didn't know who this guy was. He was there because of circumstances beyond his straight forward logic.

Because of this logic, George wasn't as eager to jump into these types of events as most of the people attending. George knew this game all too well. You get people excited about an amazing way to create $10K in ninety days and you promise them you'll tell them how to do it if they attend this 'can't miss event' and then you tell them the 'what' and you mix in a little *how* but not enough to completely be able to do it alone and voilà! You make your $10K program offer. This wasn't George's first rodeo.

George and the rest of the attendees weren't there by accident. They were all drawn to this particular event intentionally and with a purpose. Long before George ever contemplated attending this event and listening to the speaker, the speaker's marketing team was at work behind the scenes using targeted marketing to speak directly to the majority of the people in the room. Demographics, behaviors and interest are the new currency needed to build a successful online business and then turn that into online/offline engagement leading to a live event and a big ticket sales offer.

If you want to fill seats with the right people, the people that want to buy your solution, you'll need to know how to market to those people and their friends. That's what the speaker's marketing team did and it's how George found himself in the room eagerly awaiting to discover the promise.

***

"I want you to promise yourself that you will take seven things you learn today and put them into action right now. Not just write them down or take a picture of the slides but to genuinely make an action plan that you will follow up on and follow through with. This will get your online business moving within the next twenty-one days." The speaker paused and observed the crowd as they all nodded their heads in agreement.

"Now I want you to take your notepads and down the side of the first page write the numbers one to seven, leaving four lines of space between each number. Then turn the page. As I go through the lessons and insights today, you're going to take notes and whenever you hear something that you think will help you move your business along faster and in a better way, return to the front page and add it to your list until you have seven action items." The speaker watched the crowd actively write down the instructions with the seriousness of achievement on their faces.

"This is where people go wrong when they attend these live events," he continued.

George had just had this same conversation with his best friend, Dwayne, as they drove to the event. His best friend was notorious for attending these types of events, becoming highly motivated and inspired but never reaching the full potential promised. Even when he purchased the expensive coaching and mentoring packages, he still never realized a solid return on his investment.

George truly believed his good friend suffered from FOMO.

***

7 Minutes, 7 Hours and 7 Days Ago

George's phone buzzed. He just got a DM from his best friend Dwayne.

Dwayne DM –Hey bruh, I just saw this amazing event coming to town next week. It's called 7 Ways to Create More Money Using My Proven Online Business Strategy. I signed up and I can bring a guest for free. Do you want to go?

As George read the message all he could think was, *Not again,* chuckling as he pictured his friend sitting front row with his wallet in his hand, ready to make it rain like he was at the Gentlemen's Club.

George DM – Who is running this event? And when is it? Where is it? And how is this going to help me?

Dwayne DM – It's Terrell Jonson. He's a big time motivational speaker and he's launched all kinds of super successful online businesses. He's going to show us how to create a successful online business from start to launch. It's next Saturday from 8 a.m. to 6 p.m. in Toronto.

George DM – This is short notice and I don't know if I can swing it. Plus, I already have a pretty good online business. What's the rush?

Dwayne DM – It's a flash sale. It was sold out but they added a few more seats. I don't want to miss out.

George quickly recalled FOMO: the Fear of Missing Out, as he laughed to himself and thought, *I don't really want to go but I do drag him to my stuff all the time. .* He truly felt like this was going to be a real waste of time and he valued his Saturdays as he appreciated there are only fifty-two Saturdays in a year and some of those are non-negotiable due to holidays, birthdays, weddings and funerals; the ones that are left are like gold.

He glanced at the time, it was eleven minutes after eleven and suddenly he felt the urge to say yes.

Dwayne was excited. Seven minutes, seven hours and seven days later, George found himself in a room full of driven entrepreneurs listening to the charismatic Terrell Jonson.

***

The speaker, Ty, continued, "I was just like you a few years ago. Okay maybe it was many years ago now - when I had more hair!"

The participants laughed as Ty lifted his cool guy hat off his head to show off his completely bald cranium.

"But I started out no differently than you. I would attend all the seminars and workshops I could. Free ones and paid ones. Some of them were really great while others were not so great but they all had one thing in common. Do you want to know what that one thing was?"

Of course we do, George thought, but he was still listening with anticipation to what Ty would say next.

"It was me. I kept showing up the same way. Just gathering more and more information.

Looking for that perfect piece. That elusive success tip. That one key technique. That sign that would read, Hey moron, it's time to start!"

Everyone laughed. Ty was a seasoned vet. He knew people loved to laugh at the successful speaker when they self-deprecate. It brings them down off a pedestal and helps make them more relatable.

"I was stuck in a cycle because I thought I wasn't ready until one day I was talking to my mentor and he said, 'You know when I first started I had no idea what I was doing.' That's what he told me and I'm thinking to myself, *Well I hope you know what you're doing now because I'm paying you more than I make in a month to help me get going!*"

Again the room filled with laughter as they pictured Ty and his mentor having this conversation.

"Then he said, 'The only thing I knew for sure was I had to start and fail to begin to win' and that really stuck with me. I wrote it down and I posted it on my mirror. Every morning I would read that Post-it. It became my call to action. Just that simple statement made me realize I was the only one that could decide when it was time to start. My mentor was there to help me see the best way to start and what to avoid but I was the one that decides to start. And I quickly understood this very important thing that I want to share with you right now. Who wants to hear this nugget?"

It appeared that everyone in the room desperately wanted to hear this nugget Including George and Dwayne.

"You should write this one down: 'There are many keys to success so you better get yourself a key ring.'"

Some groaned and some chuckled but everyone wrote it down.

"I know it's cheesy but it's true. This is why I wanted you to make the promise to yourselves. I'm going to share at least seven real value-adding tips and techniques you can use right away for your business. Some of you will write down different ones because you're not all at the same level in your businesses and that's okay. But all of you will gain something that you can turn into a greater success but only if you take action toward that success. Does that make sense?"

Ty took a drink of his water as he watched the crowd agree with him.

George was a skeptic at heart but he found himself writing in his notebook too. He looked at Dwayne who smirked and knew better than to say anything.

Ty changed the PowerPoint slide to a blank black screen. He drew the attention of his participants and then asked another question.

"So let's get into it. Does anyone know the seven key elements for success?"

Someone yelled, "Money!"

The room filled with quiet laughter and excitement.

"Yes, money is important. What else?"

"Time!" yelled another voice.

"Very good. What else?"

"Skills!" someone suggested.

"I like this room. What else?"

Dwayne spoke up, "People?"

Ty laughed, "Is that a question or an answer?"

Dwayne smiled, "An answer," this time speaking with confidence.

"Great. What else?"

"Dedication!" someone proclaimed.

"These are all great answers and I will show you how close you are to the answers on my slides but there's a key one that I haven't yet heard."

"Luck?" asked the next voice, in response to the laughter in the room.

"No, not luck. Luck is not measurable or repeatable. It may happen from time to time but it's not something you can create, but you're close."

"Opportunity," George yelled with unusual enthusiasm.

"Yes, very good. I said there are seven key elements for success so let's look at our list and see how we did. We have:

1 – Time

2 – Money

3 – Dedication, which was close but let's change it to Resilience

4 – People, which was also close but let's call it Connections/Influencers

5 – Skills

6 – Opportunity

Looks like we're still missing one more folks. What's missing from our list?"

"Your why!" a voice bellowed.

"That's a good one and definitely important to keep you focused and motivated but it's not actually a key element for success. It's the driver for success. What else do you guys have?"

"Conditions," someone stated from the front of the room.

"Getting closer. Keep trying"

"A mentor," offered from way in the back of the room.

"Yes, that's important but that is part of connections and influencer. Keep trying."

"Investors," proposed a brave voice.

"Well, that's money and connections and opportunity. Come on people, there's something that needs to be on this list and without it, it's almost impossible to succeed. What is it?"

George was feverishly thinking but drawing a blank as was the rest of the group. They were throwing out all kinds of ideas, some repeating the categories already listed but in different forms.

Finally Ty revealed his list on the PowerPoint slide and everyone read each one out loud as he revealed them, like from an episode of Family Feud.

1 – Time

2 – Money

3 – Connections/Influencers

4 – Opportunities

5 – Skills

6 – Resilience

7 – Preparedness

A lot of chatter began once this was revealed. Dwayne said to George, "I was going to say that one but I wasn't sure."

George laughed, "Sure you were bud. Sure you were!"

Dwayne laughed too. They knew each other well.

"So what do all of these things have in common? What is the glue that makes all of these work in your journey to success?" Ty asked as he made eye contact with those in the middle of the room.

George thought for a moment. *Is it me? Is it action? Is it perseverance?* George wasn't sure what it was and didn't want to sound foolish so he sat and waited, as did everyone in the room.

"No one knows what these seven keys to success have in common? Really?" Ty wasn't really surprised, he was just playing with the participants.

"It's me!" someone yelled.

Ty smiled, "It's not you. It's your mindset. It's what you allow yourself to believe you can have and do that will enable you to utilize all seven of these whenever you need them."

"You see, I used to struggle with many of these. Creating connections, finding opportunities, building my skills, and finding the money to invest in my personal success. Until one day while speaking with my mentor he told me this story."

A Story Within a Story

Every day the student would turn to the master for instructions and permission to move forward with their skills and development and each day the master would give them a new task to achieve their quest for greatness.

This went on for months and the student was happy at the rapid progress they were making. The student was accelerating at a unique pace and the master was very happy.

One day the student asked, "What will I do today Master?" anxiously awaiting the new instructions.

"Nothing," the master responded.

"But I am ready Master. I want to learn more and more. Certainly I am not finished!?" The student was deeply concerned.

"You have gone far enough for now. Be happy with where you are at and what you have learned so far," the master replied in a cold and uncaring voice.

"No Master, I can't be done now, I've come so far so quickly already."

"You've gone far enough for now." The master was firm in their reply.

The student was upset and disappointed and thought the master was impressed with their progress. The student couldn't understand why the master wanted to stop the training all of a sudden. So the student went back to the master and declared, "If you don't want to continue to train me then I will find someone who will! I have the skills to go much further than where I am now and I will not stop or let you hold me back!"

The master stood there with a huge smile on their face. And with joy in their words, asked, "Do you believe in yourself so much that you are ready to strive with or without me?"

The student thought for a moment. They felt deep in their gut that they could do it even if they must by themself. The student could see the end result, the success of it like a movie playing in their mind. Gone was the fear of not reaching it and gone was the need to have the approval of the master.

"Yes, I believe I can," the student confidently replied.

"Believe or know?" demanded the master.

"I know I can. I believe in myself!" declared the student to the master and to the world.

"Then you have passed today's lesson. Your mind and your heart must be in sync with your self-belief to achieve your true greatness. You must know that you are ready beyond anyone else's opinion or approval before you can have true success. I am proud of you my student for many never reach this plateau."

And at that moment the student knew the importance of believing in one's self.

***

George's mind was filled with the pictures of being the student and fulfilling his dreams on his own terms. In his mind he journeyed back to a time when he had struggled to move forward in his job feeling like his boss was holding him back. He'd wished he had known the story of the student when he was younger and more ambitious.

"So it doesn't matter if it is skills, money, connections, opportunity, resilience, time or preparedness that you are working on. Until you believe in yourself none of these will really work for you." Ty took time to look at the participants in the eyes including George, who was beginning to feel a deeper connection to Ty and his words of wisdom.

"As we go through the training today, I'm going to refer to each of these and how to use them to create your online business. Does that sound good?" Ty knew he needed to keep the room fully engaged. The participants nodded in agreement and Ty continued.

"So how many of you have game-changing momentum in your business right now?" as he raised his hand but no one else raised their hand with him.

He watched as people started whispering amongst themselves.

Ty changed the slide to a picture of a pretty woman with a huge smile on her face, sitting at a computer.

"Before you can have this result, the feeling of abundance and success, you need to get people to pay attention to you." This was a lesson Ty had struggled with when he had first launched his business.

"It doesn't matter what your business is. It doesn't matter if it's an MLM business or real estate or if you're an author, a light worker, a coach. It doesn't matter. What matters is why should someone work with you or buy from you?" Ty looked at George then Dwayne.

George wasn't sure if he was supposed to answer or if it was a rhetorical question. He decided not to answer.

"So tell me, why should anyone buy from you or hire you? What makes you unique?" Ty was asking a question.

"I have vast knowledge and experience," someone said.

"So does everyone else! What else?" He was challenging his participants.

"I have solutions no one else has," someone else shouted.

"So do I. So what? Everyone claims to have the secret solution!" George was really starting to like this guy because he was saying exactly what George was thinking.

"What makes you unique? What makes you stand out?" Ty wasn't playing around. He was going to force his participants to get real and dig deep to find the answer.

"My price is lower than everyone else's!" This one came from the back of the room.

"So you don't have as much to offer or what you have to offer isn't worth much. Is that really the thing you want to be known for?" Ty was harsh.

"Come on people. Think for a moment. Why is it that you buy from the companies and people you do and not from the other people that are trying to get your attention?" He was prodding them to broaden their thinking.

George started to think about it. He thought about how he loved to buy from certain stores because he could ask questions and get answers right away. They would walk him through how things worked and what to avoid. And they would talk about the different options and price points to make sure he was getting the best value for what he wanted to spend.

George suddenly had the answer: "It's the relationship, the personal touch that you can't get anywhere else."

Ty stopped and looked at him. "Great answer. What's your name?"

"George!"

"Give George a big round of applause everyone."

The room applauded and George felt joy and a smattering of embarrassment at the same time.

"It's the relationship that makes you stand out. It's how you talk to people online and offline. It's your openness and willingness to help. It's your accessibility. It's the feel of your social media. It's the way you show up." Ty paused momentarily.

"I used to show up like a hot mess just trying to sell, sell, sell. I thought, *I'm awesome, everyone should want to buy from me!* Yeah, I was that guy. I admit it." Ty laughed at himself and the participants laughed with him.

"But that's how most of us start out. We think that what we have and what we know is so spectacular that people should reach into their pocket right away without hesitation. We think they should do this even if they don't know who we are." Ty smiled and raised his hand.

"Who's done that before?" Everyone laughed and up went hands.

"So before we can sell anything we need to create credibility and momentum. And how do you do that? You do that by sharing what you know first."

Ty's next slide showed the first offer Ty had ever made. It was a simple PDF quick guide for creating a powerful mindset shift.

George had a funny feeling. He realized he'd seen this before. This simple slide brought George back in time.

4 Trips, 4 Super Bowls and 4 Old Lang Syne's

"I'm tired of the same old B.S. from you. How many times are you going to complain about your job, complain about your coworkers, and complain about your life? You never do anything about it except complain!" His soon-to-be ex-wife was extra pissed off tonight.

George was feeling defeated. He was tired of trying. He was tired of pretending at work that he had a great marriage when he was miserable at home. He was tired of pretending to be happy making money when he felt like he was living in the movie Ground Hog Day every single day at work. He thought, *There has to be more to life than this. A loveless marriage and a bank full of money is all I have to look forward to for the rest of my life? What if I live another 60 years? Do I really have to do this for another 60 years? Can I?*

Instead of responding to his soon-to-be ex-wife, he just walked out the door, got into his car and drove to the park down the street. He got out of his car and walked to his favorite spot down by the river. He even had a favorite rock that he liked to sit on. There, he would go through his list of complaints and reasons why he should or shouldn't stay with his wife.

Even though he tried not to, a tear ran down his cheek followed by another and another until he found himself fully sobbing like a big man baby but somehow it felt good to cry, releasing emotions that he'd been swallowing for far too long.

George felt like a number one loser. He felt his life was empty and had no real value or meaning. He couldn't understand why he wasn't happy or why he couldn't make his marriage work. He used to talk about other people not being able to stay together as if he were superior to them but now the shoe was on the other foot and it didn't feel good at all.

There was something that had been on his mind for quite some time. He didn't have the courage to do it but he had often wondered if he ever got to that place how would he do it? He reached into his pocket and pulled out his phone.

He opened Google and with tear-filled eyes he started to type. And that's when it happened. It was 9:11 p.m. and what popped up was not what he thought he had typed but instead it was a video that caught his attention. This slick looking and well put together black guy started talking about feeling lost and in despair. He started telling his personal story of going from losing everything and contemplating taking his own life to suddenly discovering a video series that changed his life.

In his video, as he talked about what he went through, George could feel the emotions of the story tugging at him as if the guy was telling George's own story. At the end of the video the slick dude offered a free PDF download and video.

This changed George's life. Although it didn't save his marriage, it did give him the courage to believe he would be more than fine to walk away from both his marriage and his job. It also gave him the courage to talk to someone about how he was feeling and he soon found out he was not alone. That night was the beginning of the rest of his life.

***

George sat in awe wondering if Ty had seen the same video. Maybe the slick guy was Ty's personal mentor and possibly what had inspired Ty to create his own PDF offer. George's eyes were a little watery just thinking about that night four years ago before he quickly wiped them away so no one would notice his vulnerability.

Ty continued, "This is the first offer I created. It was based on this amazing training I had taken and the results of that training were life changing! You see, I didn't start out wearing suits and ties. Before I learned how to master my mind and create the mindset for success, my whole life was a struggle. I would get fired from one job after another. And guess what happens when you keep getting fired from your jobs?"

"You go broke?" someone from the back shouted. Everyone laughed.

"No, worse than that. The love of your life leaves you." Ty paused. "Your parents and siblings treat you like a loser." No one was laughing for they knew how true this statement was.

"But I got lucky and I found not only this information but a few mentors that wanted to help me, some for free and some for a fee." Everyone joined in a much needed laugh, helping lighten the mood of the presentation.

"But before I could create a giveaway to build up my credibility, I had to be able to answer this one question: What problem was I solving?" Ty took a sip of his water, noticing it was time for a break so people could stretch, go to the restrooms, and network.

"We're going to take a break in a second but before we do I want you to write this question down in your notepad: *What problem am I solving?* And next write down the question: *Who has this problem?* Think about the type of person who would have this problem. Where do they work? How much money do they make? What kinds of things are they interested in? Who do they know? What kinds of books do they read? What kinds of movies do they like? Really drill down, okay?" Ty nodded his head *yes* and everyone mirrored him.

"Let's take a twenty minute break. Make sure you meet at least one person you didn't know when you got here. Deal?" There was a shower of yeses as everyone got up to stretch and move around.

Dwayne turned to George and asked, "So far so good, huh?"

"Yes, I'm actually surprised and impressed. It's not what I was expecting. He's way more down to earth than I thought he'd be. Thanks for twisting my arm to get me here." George could be humble, sometimes.

"No problem buddy!" Dwayne was happy his friend was enjoying the morning.

In his not-so-good Schwarzenegger voice he exclaimed, "I'll be back!"

George headed over to the coffee dispenser to grab a mug. There was a crowd of people standing around the area chatting. He noticed a young man standing by himself so he went over to introduce himself knowing this was an opportunity to meet one new person.

"Hey my name is George, I see your badge says 'My Name is Peter.' How are you doing Peter?"

"I'm well thanks. So what do you do George?"

"Well I guess I go up to random strangers and say hi." They both laughed. "But seriously, I'm a paid assassin and I'm just here following my next mark. It's good to do your research first to see the best way to take care of business without drawing too much attention to yourself." George winked.

"I see. That's an interesting line of work. Where did you learn how to do it? Was there a class at your university?" Peter laughed hoping George was joking about his line of work. Praying, actually.

"I watched a lot of Marvel Comic movies." They both laughed. Peter's laugh was in relief.

"What brings you here, Peter?" George wanted to know this guy a bit better and kill some time while Dwayne was networking.

"Well, I'm friends with Terrell and he invited me. I started a business a while ago and he really helped me navigate the harsh truths of entrepreneurial life." Peter had a huge smile on his face.

"That's great. This is my first time seeing him. I really like it so far," George replied.

"So what do you really do George?" Peter was curious.

"You mean you don't believe I'm a highly trained assassin? What gave it away? Was it the beer belly? Damn beer belly. I always forget to suck it in when I tell that story." George was full of jokes.

"Well I was into IT and then I started my own online business buying and trading sports memorabilia." George loved doing that. "I still do IT consulting too for a few small businesses in London, Ontario."

"Wow, so you're living the dream!" Peter was excited.

"If having more time than money is living the dream then I'm your man!" They both chuckled.

Just then Dwayne found George and George introduced him to Peter.

Ty reappeared at the front of the room and asked everyone to make their way back to their seats as he was starting in a few minutes.

"I hope everyone had a good break and got to meet someone they didn't know before. What was one thing you learned about that someone?'

Peter stood up. "I met a highly trained assassin."

"Oh really, and who was that Peter?" Ty was loving this.

"It's my new friend George."

"Where are you George? Please stand up. Will the real Slim Shady please stand up?" Ty laughed as he sung the classic jam.

George reluctantly stood up to a round of applause and he couldn't help but laugh.

Ty looked him over and said, "So you're a highly trained assassin, huh?"

George quickly sucked in his beer belly and replied yes while trying to hold his breath. Laughter filled the room.

"So let me ask you, how did you come up with this story?" Ty was intrigued.

"Well I had a chance to meet a famous businessman once and he said, 'You got to say something that people will remember. Ever since then I use the assassin job as an ice breaker.'" George loved telling that story.

"Wow, this is what I'm talking about people. This is a great way to stand out and now you see everyone in the room knows who you are. Great job. Give George another round of applause."

George was starting to feel like a superstar. This kind of attention was great for his ego. He could feel his head swell more and more by the second.

"So how many of you took a moment to add some details to your list?" asked Ty as he raised his hand. Some raised their hands too.

"It's okay if you didn't. It will be part of your homework. But once you know who has the problem that you can solve and you know what they like and the real details and demographics, then you can start to talk to them in a way that will draw them to you so you can help them." Ty loves teaching this. It's what he did to fill the room today.

"This is something I learned from my mentor. This is what he taught me when I was struggling to get in front of the people that needed what I was selling. This is what he told me."

A Story Within A Story

Two men had vendor stands at a market. One was at the north end of the market and the other was at the south end. Each of them sold men's shirts and ties. But the one in the south end always had an abundance of customers and often ran out of shirts before the end of the day. The stand on the north end was never too busy and would always have shirts left over at the end of the day.

The man with the stand in the north end would always complain to the market organizers that he suffered due to the poor location: low traffic, no visibility, blaming the market organizer for his lackluster business revenue. He began to refuse to pay the rent until he got a prime location in the south end, close to his competitor.

Finally, after much debate and negotiation, he was awarded a prime location in the south end of the market, close to the other vendor. Happy with his victory, he looked forward to the first day at his new premium location.

But to his surprise the results were even worse than before. Now people would compare prices and style before making a purchase decision. They were not buying any shirts from him. He angrily blamed the other vendor, accusing them of sabotaging his business.

He ordered his son to go over to the other stand and to listen to and record what they were saying to the customers so he could prove sabotage to his business and get them kicked out of the market. His son did exactly as instructed and brought the recording back to his father so he could listen for himself.

This is what he heard, 'Hello my friend. I see you are a young entrepreneur striving for success. I see you know the value and importance of making a strong first impression for your potential clients and future customers. I want you to look at these shirts we just got in and imagine how impressive you will look wearing one to your next meeting. See in your mind for a second, your client seeing this well-dressed, successful businessman sitting across from them ready to help them with the unique solutions that only you can provide. Now hear them in your mind complimenting you on this shirt. And see in your mind right now how the waitress is looking at you as if she were seeing a rock star. Don't you want to feel like that? To make that kind of impression for your next meeting? These shirts sell fast and I only have a few in your size because I don't want everyone to have your shirt. This shirt was made for you my friend. So please try it on and see how good and impressive you'll look in it. Take a picture with your phone while you're wearing it and send it to your friends and I'm sure they will tell you the same thing I just told you. And if you buy three I'll give you 20% off the whole purchase, just don't tell anyone. I can't do this for everyone but I know you're a driven entrepreneur and I know what it's like to show up in the right way to give your client the confidence to do business with you. So I'm here to help you win that business. So let me ask you, how will you pay? Will that be credit or debit today?'

Right away the vendor knew that it wasn't the location or the competitor, it was himself. He didn't know what his customers really needed. He realized the other vendor was selling to a target market, while he was trying to sell to everyone. He could appreciate as he listened that the other vendor was selling a feeling. They were selling an image of future success. They were selling an emotion.

He also knew that young entrepreneurs weren't his market. It wasn't what he knew. He knew how to sell to older gentlemen. He knew that they sought prestige, status and respect. He knew how to sell that and the ways to evoke the feeling that they wanted when wearing a shirt. This is where his focus needed to be. This was what his business was.

The next weekend as he targeted this specific demographic, using words and phrases they understood and identified with, he had the best weekend ever at the market. He sold all his shirts and the other vendor still sold all their shirts too. From that moment on he knew the importance of knowing how to talk to his customers in a way that would speak to them emotionally and directly.

***

"There is power in the way you say things. Certain language and descriptions will speak to your target participants and get their attention while other people will not notice or care. And that's what you ultimately want: it's to talk directly to those who want to hear from you and who need to hear from you." Ty took a sip from his water bottle as he watched everyone flip back to the front of their books to take notes.

"Once you know what problem you're solving and how to communicate directly to those that need your solution, then you are ready to create a giveaway product or service. Something of value that you're going to give away for free. This is the very beginning of your sales cycle." Ty put up a slide showing the first step in the sales cycle. It was a picture of a digital product with an arrow going from the product to an email list.

"You want to offer a free digital product or service in exchange for their email address. This is the first sell and the reason it's the first sell is so they can have a sample of what it's like to work with you or to use one of your products or services." Ty knew everyone already understood the concept but most didn't know what to do with the list once they had it in place.

George absolutely hated this kind of giveaway tactic. He didn't even open his emails most of the time because it was just someone trying to sell him something he didn't want. George wasn't impressed with this part of the seminar.

Ty continued, "Now I know everyone is on someone's email list. How many of you love getting weekly and daily emails?" Ty raised his hand and very few raised their hands back. Ty laughed.

"And how many of you are on my list?"

Quite a few people raised their hands in the room.

"And how many emails do you get from me per week?" Ty asked everyone.

"Not many." Someone said.

"Do you know why?" Ty waited as the participants had to think about it for a second.

"Because you're lazy?" Everyone laughed.

"Ha ha, very funny! No it's because I know everyone is sending emails. It's becoming white noise. So how did I communicate with most of you to get you here?" Ty wanted to see if they realized what he had done to drive so many people to attend.

"I received a Messenger invite somehow," someone said near the front of the room.

"I saw an ad on Facebook," yelled another person.

"So let me tell you what happened. I posted a free giveaway offer and asked you to like, comment and share to enter. I was giving away a one hundred dollar pre-paid Visa card. Then I boosted the post using keywords based on your interests, demographics, region and behaviors. I had over 3,000 entries. All those who entered went straight to an opt-in page for my Messenger list and voila! I marketed this seminar directly to you because I knew this is what you were interested in: building a stronger online business and I had the solutions you needed." Ty smiled as he watched the participants react to this technique.

George was also smiling because he could see the more targeted method of communication. It is more personal and inviting than an email. George's interest was once again peaked and engaged.

"Never think that there is only one way to do things or only one way to become successful. Remember at the beginning of the day I told you that you would need a key ring for success?"

The participants smiled and whispered amongst themselves for a moment as they remembered the statement.

"The product you offer should solve a small problem right away for your target audience. You must solve it as promised, completely. No snake oil tricks. No upsells to get the solution. You can upsell additional information in regards to the bigger problem but you must solve the first problem for free as advertised. This is very important. Mess this up and you've lost your customer forever!" Ty was sharing a harsh truth of business.

George knew this all too well. He had unknowingly experienced this mistake many times. He'd signed up for something and only received half the solution then had to dump big bucks into getting the real full solution. This was one of the main reasons he'd lost trust in these weekend seminar events.

George felt that this time was different. He felt that Ty was revealing the secrets to running a great seminar and building an authentic business. It is a trust building up with Ty, a trust that he'd never really felt with other presenters he'd met.

Ty changed the slide. This one was an interesting picture of a successful looking man having fun chatting with people at a bar. The man was dressed to impress and everyone around him seemed happy that he was there speaking with them.

"You see, you need to tell a story with your content. Whenever people see your post on social media it's an opportunity to build engagement, credibility, product confidence and awareness. All this can be achieved with a single picture and the right caption. So what caption do you think should go with this picture?" Ty looked directly at Dwayne until Dwayne looked away.

"Anyone want to take a swing at it?" Ty looked at the suddenly shy and timid participants.

"I guess we don't have any marketers in the room. If you don't know how to do this, it's okay. Just make sure you have hiring someone to write great captions for you in your business budget." Ty chuckled because he understood how money solves most skills lacking in business.

"I would write, *I have so much fun meeting interesting people and sharing ideas with them. But it wasn't always like this for me. I used to struggle to even approach people, but once I developed my mindset hacks and my success habits, I had the confidence to show up in my greatness and thrive. Imagine what you could do with this kind of confidence?* Or something along those lines. And I would finish it off with, *If you want to learn more, like and comment 'yes' and I will send you some details.*" He paused for a moment. "See how powerful that can be? The picture shows success and then I'm letting people know I have the solution that they need to achieve their greatness and thrive. The language only speaks to those who really and truly want these results. Now the trick is to post a wide variety of cool content that drives the same message in different ways and wording. This is how you engage your participants and help them understand that you have the solutions they need." Ty was giving them a strong base for building a successful online business campaign.

George was writing it down but Ty was talking too fast for him to catch everything and he wasn't the only one struggling to take notes at the speed of light. Ty repeated it a few times until everyone was finished writing.

"Think for a second about what kind of story you want to tell with your marketing and engagement. What do people need to know about your business? What do they need to know about your success? What are the feelings you want them to have? What is the future they can achieve if they learn what you have to offer? What's your lifestyle, your method of engagement? I know some of you have issues with posting your success. You are afraid to be successful or to show it. But think about this. Why would someone want to buy from you if you can't show them the results of what you actually do? If they only see your product and your product has helped you improve your life, how are they supposed to know that if you don't show them your actual results? You have to show them how it feels to succeed. Show them how it feels to have the results that you are experiencing now. Let them see the feeling of having it!" Ty knew this was a hurdle for so many entrepreneurs. He knew it was an important message and watched as everyone wrote it down.

This was something George had struggled with too.

7 Months, 7 Days Off and 7 Meetups Ago

The money was finally starting to flow on a consistent basis from his online landing pages and from his consulting business. George finally had extra money, and a lot of it, so he decided it was time to get himself a new car.

He called his friend Dwayne to see if he wanted to go test drive some nice cars and Dwayne excitedly agreed, so George jumped into his old car and headed to his friend's house to pick him up.

"Where are we going first?" asked Dwayne.

"The Ford Dealership, then Dodge," George proudly said.

Dwayne looked at him for a moment in confusion. "Not Cadillac, Audi, Benz, or maybe Jaguar?"

"They're nice cars but they're too flashy for me. I don't want people to think I'm rich," George explained.

"But aren't you rich? Didn't you work hard to build your business for all these years? Struggled actually to get to a place where you can treat yourself to the type of car you deserve? And now you want to downplay it? To play small?" Dwayne didn't get where George was coming from.

"But I don't need it. It's not me." George was getting a little defensive.

"Come on George. You've been talking about owning a Caddy for years. You want it and you deserve it. Plus it doesn't show gratitude for the blessing you've been given if you don't reward yourself once in a while. It's like you're saying you don't need all these blessings. Then if they get taken away from you, you'll be upset that they're gone but the whole time you had them you didn't show appreciation for them. They were given to you for a reason. So what energetic messages are you really sending?" Dwayne was learning a lot about the importance of recognizing abundance and showing gratitude and giving thanks when it comes into your life instead of pushing it away or not fully accepting it.

George was silent. He was deep in thought, trying to figure out if Dwayne was preaching greed or if he was truly talking about accepting and acknowledging the blessings that were coming to him.

He had always dreamed about owning a Cadillac, seeing himself behind the wheel, turning on the engine and listening to it hum, adjusting the mirrors and the seats to his comfort, and turning up the sound system, blasting some Led Zeppelin. He always felt successful and accomplished whenever he visited this picture in his mind. Whenever he felt this experience in his heart, all the emotions of having this car were the same emotions he imagined a football team felt winning a championship.

"You're right Dwayne. I've always wanted a Caddy. Why would I settle for less now that I can afford one? It's like I've been given what I asked for over and over again for so many years and now that I can finally have it, I'm saying, *No thanks.* What was I thinking?"

That day George and Dwayne went to the Cadillac dealership and test drove several models. At the end of the day he bought a Cadillac CT6-V sport and he was filled with gratitude as he signed the papers.

***

"Most people that struggle to build success have a poor mentality about money. They see having money as a form of greed, as a negative accomplishment instead of seeing it as the fruit of their labor. It's simply compensation for an exchange of greater value." Ty reached into his pocket and took out a one hundred dollar bill. He held it up above his head for everyone to see.

"We all want more money but even when money comes our way we often turn the other way." Ty walked slowly from the front of the room toward the back of the room as he talked while holding the one hundred dollar bill above his head.

"We say, *I want to be rich, I want more money, I need more money.* But when it is right in front of us, what do we do? We watch as it passes us by, even when it's right in front of us." Ty was approaching George's seating area.

George had a sudden feeling to do something he would never imagine himself doing. He felt the compelling urge to step out of his comfort zone and seize the moment. As Ty was walking by, George jumped up and snatched the one hundred dollar bill from Ty's hand.

Ty looked at him and smiled, "I see the highly trained assassin knows how to recognize an opportunity when it's right in front of him. Congratulations my friend, you just made one hundred dollars!" Everyone cheered and clapped as George sat back down in surprise. He never expected that Ty would let him keep the one hundred dollar bill. He still couldn't believe it as he sat down and played the moment back to himself in his mind.

"You see, you have to be prepared to take action when an opportunity comes to you. You need to be aware of what you are asking. When you think about your success and learn how to see it because when it shows up, it never shows up in the exact way you planned." This was a lesson Ty had learned through trial and error. He came to realize that you only need to focus on the *what* and put into motion things that could bring the *what* to you and then see which one develops in a way that brings you to your *what*.

"Let me ask you this: what is an opportunity? What does that word mean to you? How do you see it?" Ty looked around the room.

"A way to succeed," someone said.

"The way to get what you want," replied another voice.

"The answer to your struggle," yelled someone from the back of the room.

"Let me tell you what it really is." Ty continued, "It's just a possibility. It's something you could do if you're prepared to take action. If you don't have the confidence or the resources to act on it then it's nothing more than something you could have done. An opportunity is only a possibility unless you add action to it."

Ty watched as this harsh truth sunk into the minds of the participants. He took a sip of his water and continued.

"You see, it doesn't matter what skills you have if you don't act. Doesn't matter how much you know. Whether you have enough money to do it or not, that doesn't matter. Who you know doesn't matter either. Nothing matters if the opportunity comes to you and you can't recognize it or you're not prepared to act on it. Do you see how important it is to be prepared?"

Ty surveyed the crowd and observed that most of them were writing in their note pads and so he repeated the statement again.

George was writing too. He knew this, he had heard it before but the one hundred dollar bill really resonated with him. It was proof that opportunities pass him by all the time because most opportunities are not as obvious as a guy walking around waving a one hundred dollar bill in the air waiting for someone to grab it from them. The point was definitely made.

"So the question is, how do you prepare for opportunities and how do you know when they're the right ones for you? This is something I asked my mentor and this is what he told me."

A Story Within A Story

"How does the bear know where to find the fish? When should they go and get the fish? How does the bird know in what direction to fly? When it is time to land? Neither the bear nor the bird can read. They cannot write instructions down. They cannot speak, so how do they know?" The mentor was wise beyond words.

"How do any of the animals survive and thrive without words, language, or symbols?"

"They are in tune with their gut feelings. They are guided by simple logic and natural wisdom. They use all of their senses and are guided by things beyond their own understanding." The mentor stopped talking and sat deep in thought for what seemed to be eternity.

The student sat quietly too, waiting for the next words of wisdom, for the rest of the thought. The mentor took his time not because he was searching for the words but to let the student learn how to ponder such things in silence

After some time, just the right amount of time, the mentor continued the lesson.

"They are not distracted by language and opinions of others. There is no debate as to what the best way is to catch the fish. In what direction to fly. Where the prime place is to get the best fish. Where the birds should land. Why the bear shouldn't eat the fish but instead eat the berries and roots.

The bear wants the fish; the bird wants to fly to their destination and they are both focused on getting the fish, finding the land. All their senses are focused on this one goal. All their thoughts are aligned with accomplishing this one thing. Eating the fish. Finding the land. Once that is complete then they focus on the next goal for that day."

The mentor looked at the student in anticipation of questions or a quarrel. The student was also pondering the simplistic existence of the bear and the bird, wondering how it related to the complex life of a human. *Surely the mentor was not suggesting that all we have to do is think about the basic needs. We have far more things to do in life than eat and sleep,* the student thought.

"But mentor, we are advanced for a reason. We can accomplish far more than just survival. How does this relate to the human experience?" The student was very unsure.

"Before you can have what you want, you need to see yourself having it. You have to feel what it will be like to have it. You have to listen to your gut feelings and learn to act on them even if your logic is telling you otherwise. You must learn to filter out the distractions and opinions of others for they are not walking the path you are. You must learn to quiet your mind and feel the path of your success in all its hidden journeys."

The mentor sat again in silence but the student didn't wait to ask the most important question of the day, "But how do I do this mentor?"

"With practice!" And the mentor stood up and walked away. The lesson was finished and the student had their next assignment: to practice focusing on success using all their senses and letting their gut feelings, their intuition, guide them.

***

Ty looked at the time. It was time to break for lunch. He already knew it was time as his stomach was starting to rumble but he was impressed by how engaged the participants were.

"I want you to think about what we've discussed as we break for lunch. We're going to take an hour and fifteen minutes so you can get some food energy, network and enjoy a walk outside. Make sure you're back on time. I'm giving away one android tablet to one lucky guest but you have to be in the room to win. This is my way of making sure you all come back on time for the afternoon session. And don't forget that we have a guest speaker joining us by Skype this afternoon too. So enjoy your lunch break and we'll see you back here in one hour and fifteen minutes."

Everyone stood up and the room instantly filled with the sounds of random conversations. George and his friend took a much needed stretch and decided to leave the hotel conference room and look for a nice bar and grill for lunch.

As they walked to the car discussing the many concepts they had just heard throughout the morning, George's eye caught the eye of a pretty girl.

He smiled and as he was going to look away she said, "You must be the luckiest and worst assassin in the world." She had a huge smile on her face as she joked with George. At that moment George realized he'd forever be known as the highly trained assassin to this group.

"Well I never claimed to be good at it," he replied. "I'm more of an IT assassin." Comedy wasn't George's strong suit.

"I'm really loving this seminar so far. I learned a lot about things, more than just building an online business." She seemed friendly and full of energy.

"My name is Cheryl but I guess you can see that from my name tag and I know your name is George and is this your partner?" Cheryl was curious.

"This is my partner in crime Dwayne. We grew up together," George nervously blurted out as he felt intimidated when talking with pretty women. Dwayne had a puzzled look on his face but didn't say anything although he'd only actually known George for the past seven years. He thought a nervous lie never killed anyone, at least not instantly.

"I'm waiting for my friend but she's busy networking and I'm starving. Where are you guys going for lunch?" George could tell that Cheryl was more than comfortable around people she didn't know and her kind tone melted his nervousness away.

"Well, we're looking for a bar and grill, somewhere casual where the music is a little too loud for lunch and the beer is cold." As he said it he subconsciously sucked in his belly a little bit.

Cheryl smiled brightly, "I know the perfect place. I'll show you if we can get a ride with you?"

George was more than happy to have Cheryl and her friend join him and Dwayne for lunch. Dwayne wasn't so sure. He didn't know what his wife would think if she saw pictures on social media of him with George and two pretty women but he could see that George was enjoying himself for the first time in a long time and so he was willing to risk it for his friend. *Besides,* he thought, *it's only lunch!*

Lunch consisted of the normal *What do you do, What do you love, Why are you here* type of conversation. Cheryl's friend was also married so Dwayne felt much more comfortable. George was feeling an energy he hadn't felt for some time but he was certain Cheryl was only interested in chatting. He was pretty sure he'd never see her again after this event so he kept from going into any detail about his personal life. The conversation was mainly about business goals and dreams which they all had plenty of.

The ladies decided to visit the restroom and Dwayne turned to George as soon as they left and asked with a big goofy smile on his face, "So my friend, what do you think of Cheryl?"

"I think I just met my future ex-wife!" George blurted out.

"Well, I guess so with that attitude. You might as well give her half your money right now. It's that kind of negativity and low self-esteem that sabotages any and every potential good relationship that comes your way!" Dwayne was a little angry because he still felt he was taking a bit of a risk just having lunch with other women..

"I'm sorry, you're right. I should be positive and filled with gratitude that I didn't have to spend the whole lunch break looking at your ugly face!" They both laughed.

"That's more like it," Dwayne replied with a chuckle.

"But seriously, Cheryl has a wonderful personality and she's not hard to look at either, but come on, you haven't seen me without my shirt on. She's out of my league my friend." George really did have some self-love issues.

"Buddy, I've seen you at the beach, but that's superficial. She doesn't seem like that kind of stuff is that important to her. If it was, she wouldn't have started talking to you in the first place genius!" Dwayne was always hitting George with common sense logic.

"Well don't get your wedding suit out yet. My heart's not ready for another crushing. I'm still trying to put it back together from the last time." You could hear the sadness in George's voice.

"Man, you've been divorced for years. It's time to move on!" Dwayne shook his head.

"No, not her. You forgot about Tracey already!" George was surprised. Tracey really did a number on him. That one cut deep to the core and almost sent him into a full depression.

"Damn! I tried to block that one out of my head!" She almost sent Dwayne into a depression too and he was only a witness to what had transpired.

Just then the ladies returned. George looked at his watch, "We better get moving. We don't want to miss the giveaway!"

"I was just thinking the same thing!" Cheryl remarked.

George treated everyone to lunch, picking up the tab. They then made their way back to the conference room.

***

Ty was getting everything ready. He had a bowl full of ticket stubs so he could draw a number for the prize: the android tablet. The room started filling quickly and the chatter was building. There seemed to be real excitement about winning the tablet even though most people already had one and didn't even use it. Still, people were rushing back for their chance to win. It was a proven strategy that Ty always used to make sure people returned for the second half.

Ty drew the number and someone near the front of the room won. It was time to start the second half of the seminar.

"We've outlined what you need to think about to get your business up and going. Those are all important steps to create credibility, engagement and trust. But to create real momentum and stability you will need two things. Does anyone know what they are?" Ty looked around the room but everyone looked too full from lunch to answer.

"Daily routines and the daily tasks needed to reach your goals. How many of you have daily routines right now?" Ty raised his hand above his head and some people raised their hand too.

"And how many of you have daily tasks?" The raised hands were less than they were for the first question.

"Okay, I'm going to talk about both of them. But first let me say this: there are many great ways to create daily routines and daily tasks. The key is to find the way that resonates with you. This means you'll have to undergo some trial and error, okay?"

George immediately thought back to the time he tried to create a daily routine. What a disaster that was. He was only consistent for the first few days and then he'd miss a day here and there until he found himself back on the same old routine he had been on so he wasn't expecting to hear anything he hadn't already heard before.

Ty put a slide up of an old beat up notebook with tattered edges and a torn front cover. The notebook looked ragged and worn out. "This was my old notebook and within these pages are written the habitual routines that I had tried and failed at over the years. I used to jump on the latest trendy ones and a lot of them worked for a while but others were 100% pure crap. Just like the person seeking that magical diet, I tried them all, but nothing would stick. Who has been there?"

Everyone raised their hand in acknowledgement.

"It wasn't until I did one main thing that allowed me to change how my habits would work for me. I started looking at how it would fit into what I was doing and if it would enhance my routine or simply be changing it." Ty advanced the slide to a young woman sitting in a classic meditation pose.

"I had a conversation with my mentor Guru Modziw. I know it's a hard name to pronounce. I would call him Guru M for short or just Guru. We were talking one day about my notebook and all of the various routines people teach to achieve success and create consistent results in life and he said this: 'It is not the routine that is important but why you are doing the routine that's important. Before you wish for a great routine, you must first know what you want the routine to accomplish. Many people wake up at 5 a.m. but they don't really know why they are up at 5 a.m. they think it is to meditate or to exercise, or to think deeply. But it is not.' And then he just stopped talking. I was losing my mind and thinking, *Come on Guru, don't leave me hanging! Tell me why it's important to get up at 5 a.m.*"

Everyone was laughing as Ty told the story and then George asked, "So what is the reason? Don't leave us hanging!" His comedy muscle was getting slightly stronger.

Ty smiled. "Wouldn't it be horrible if the story ended there? What if my Guru had just gotten up and left me to figure it out? That's the kind of stuff he would do to me all the time. But I asked him to elaborate and this is what he said, 'There are four states of restful mind. They are beta, alpha, theta, and delta. *Beta* is for conversations. Alpha is for meditation and reflection. Theta is for day dreaming and to tap into the subconscious mind. Delta is for the deep sleep state of dreaming. Your body naturally regulates these states as a system and as day turns to night you will naturally move from one state to the other. The important thing to know is that by 10 p.m. you should be in theta thinking about what you want to accomplish as if you have already experienced it. Now this in itself is common knowledge but the key to it is that if you go to sleep by 10 p.m., you will be ready to wake up at 5 a.m. and from 5 a.m. to 7 a.m. your mind will be in theta. This is when you are most able to speak directly to your subconscious mind, to program it for the day, week or year. Each morning you are to use this time to fill your mind with the things you want to experience, to build your belief, your skills and anything else you feel is necessary for your subconscious to know and do.' That's what he told me. I sat there trying to get my head around it, wondering why I had never heard this explanation before. Was it real or just another test?" Ty was posing this as a question to the participants too.

"I've heard this explanation before too," someone called out.

"So have I," someone else added.

Ty spoke, "Yes. Once I did some research, I realized a lot of people knew about this but not everyone. Some were just getting up at 5 a.m. because they'd heard that's the time successful people get up and go for a jog!" Everyone chuckled at Ty's statement.

"So I started to understand that affirmations were important but the mind-state that you practice them in is just as important. The routine has to have a definite purpose to create the result wanted and the result needs to be something you want to experience now. So for you to really be able to create a great routine, you must first learn how to bring your mind into the theta state. This is why so many successful people meditate and say affirmations before the crack of dawn. It's because their mind is already in the prime state for the subconscious to absorb the information and the new reality you want to create for yourself." Ty took a drink of water.

He could see everyone was frantically writing down his words. He went back over the key points and showed the slides that matched what he was saying.

"To start building a great routine you first have to decide what big life changing goal you'd like to accomplish in the next five years. Write it down now. Now add some details to it. What you need to do is create a mind movie where you're the star. How will you feel once you've accomplished this life changing goal? Who will be there with you? Where will you be when you accomplish it? Add as much detail as you can right now. And here's the hurdle most of you will run into right away. You're going to start thinking about something like becoming a world-wide bestselling author and you're going to say to yourself, *But how would I do that or I can't do that.* Stop! You don't have to have any clue how you will do it. As a matter of fact, if you already know how you will do it then the five-year goal is not life changing. You're thinking too small. I want you to really allow yourself to dream. It is very important that you pick something that scares you to say aloud because if you say it aloud people will think you're crazy. That's what I want you to write down. Work on it for the next five minutes and then we will continue."

George really had to think about what he really wanted to accomplish in the next five years. He had so many ideas but as soon as he started to think about them he would automatically try to work out how he would do it, try to figure out how he could make it possible. He was really struggling to even allow himself to dream at the size Ty told them to dream. He thought to himself, *Isn't that crazy, I can't even let myself picture my dream life! Even my dream life is rooted in the limits of my current reality. Dreaming big is not as easy as it sounds.*

George glanced at his friend Dwayne who was writing a novel. Then he looked around and observed that most people were filling their pages with details. George jotted a few things down and decided he'd go into more detail tomorrow when he had time to look over his notes and reflect on everything he was learning today.

After a few more minutes passed, Ty returned to the front of the room. He was ready to give them additional instructions on how to create a routine.

"Here is the key to what you have just written down. No matter what time you get up, make sure you wake up forty-five minutes to one hour earlier than you do right now. Chose a time and be consistent with this time. You will need to do three things during this time:

1. Give gratitude for the things in your life.
2. Think about and connect to the feelings of your life changing five-year goal, and play it like a movie in your mind.
3. Listen to affirmations or say affirmations.

"Leave time to do all three things. At least forty- five minutes and don't forget to do some deep rhythmic breathing to help create the theta. Also, stretch and move your body. If you can take a walk while you do your affirmations, then do that. Just make sure you're consistent with your routine and don't worry about the results. This routine will have a positive effect and if you know anything about compound interest, then you'll understand the importance of consistent daily action."

Ty looked at everyone and could see that they needed a break from writing.

"We are going to have our special guest Skype in to speak to us about 7 Essential Mindset Hacks Every Driven Entrepreneur Needs in a few minutes, so let's take a quick five-minute break while we get things set up. But please don't take more than five minutes. I don't want you to miss our guest speaker's presentation, okay?" Everyone nodded in agreement and started to move around the room.

George went to get himself a fresh cup of afternoon coffee. There was a line up so he chatted with some people in the line as he waited his turn. He was feeling excited and a little overwhelmed with what he was learning. He was thinking about how realistic it would be for him to get up forty-five minutes earlier than he already was each morning.

He got his coffee and went outside for some fresh air. As he stood there enjoying the sun peeking through the clouds and bathing him with a few rays, he saw her. Cheryl was outside sitting on a nearby bench looking at her phone. He decided to walk over and strike up a conversation.

As he approached her, he could see she had a stressed and concerned look on her face as she typed feverishly into her phone. She wasn't looking joyful and perky like she had earlier so he quickly reached into his pocket to get out his phone and pretended he'd just received a message. This was his way of aborting the mission of starting up a conversation with Cheryl. Just as he turned around to run to safety, Cheryl called out to him.

"Hey, Mr. Assassin. Come sit with me for a second. I could use a man's perspective at the moment and a friendly voice too." George wasn't sure what kind of domestic quarrel he was about to referee but he knew he wasn't qualified to give any useful advice.

"Hey Cheryl. I saw you sitting there but I could see you were busy with something so I thought I'd give you privacy." He wanted to explain why he was about to abandon her, half hoping he still could.

"No, I'm glad you're here. I just had a text conversation with my brother. He is so hard on himself and he's so down. I was struggling to cheer him up. He just broke up with his long-term girlfriend and also recently lost his job. I'm afraid he is falling into a dark place." Cheryl's voice was starting to crack a little with emotions bubbling up to the surface and desperately trying to hold back.

"Wow, that's a lot all at once. It's not so easy for us when things like this happen. Men are not in the habit of talking about this kind of stuff, especially to our families." George realized he was an expert in this subject and started to think this must be the real reason he was guided to meet Cheryl in the first place.

"But we talk about everything. We're like best friends. He's always been there for all my ups and downs. He's the first one to tell me that everything's going to be okay and that everything happens for my benefit and to trust the process." She was a little frustrated with her brother.

"He's your older brother, right?" George had a suspicion.

"Yes, he's three years older than me. I have a younger sister too." Cheryl wasn't sure where George was going with this.

"So his role is to protect his sisters and be there for them. He always knows the right words to say. The ones you need to hear. He's your rock, your foundation. But what happens when he has issues? Who does he turn to? Because he is your superman, the man of steel, he might be feeling that he can't have issues and not know what to do. He needs to figure it out on his own because he's the big brother and because he's a man." George knew exactly how this felt, from experience.

"That's so stupid. Why do men think they have to be supermen? Why do they hide their emotions and struggle alone? Why don't they just let the people who love them, in?" Cheryl was becoming angry.

"Because if they admit they don't have all the answers, if they admit they are scared and they don't know what to do, they feel like they are letting everyone who is counting on them down. They feel like a real failure because none of their friends talk about their emotions. Their friends say the same thing whenever there's turmoil in their life. *Man up.* That's the only advice we get. We're somehow not allowed to have real-life problems and be vulnerable. We have to be the shoulder for everyone else to cry on. We're not even allowed to cry." This was one of the harsh truths that George had lived many times.

"That's ridiculous. Who says men can't cry? Who says men can't have emotions? Who makes these stupid rules?" Cheryl's face filled with emotion and George could see she was on the brink of tears.

"The reason you're so concerned about your brother is exactly because of these rules. You are not used to seeing him being vulnerable. You're not used to seeing him not be in control, seeing him filled with dark emotion, so your whole world is upside-down right now. You're not sure how to help him because you've never had to help him before. He's always had the answers and he's feeling like he's letting you down just by being in this situation. And so he doesn't want to talk to you about it because he still wants to be your superman." George could see that Cheryl was starting to understand the underlying issue men have when things start falling apart around them.

"So it sounds like you've had a similar experience. How did you pull yourself out of it?" Cheryl knew George had the answers.

"I tried everything I could. First drinking, yelling, fighting, driving too fast and not caring. It was a very dark time for me. I tried everything except for the one thing that could save me: I wouldn't allow myself to cry. I wouldn't allow myself to experience the grief and loss I felt. I just kept blaming myself for not being a *real man*. A *real man* wouldn't have found himself in this situation. A *real man* would be able to make his wife happy, excel at his job, make the big money and have the big house. That was my mindset until one day I just let go of being a *real man* and started to cry. I opened up those tear ducts and it was like Niagara Falls. The emotions started pouring out of me. I was releasing all the negative feelings I had about myself and the entire situation. In that moment something magical happened. I realized that crying didn't make me less of a man, it made me more human." George's voice was tender and crackled too as he held back the emotions these memories brought. It's something he seldom spoke about and never shared with a stranger.

Cheryl leaned over and gave him a huge hug as she began to cry. She whispered, "Thank you for sharing this with me" into his ear as she held on to him tightly as if he were her life line. A small tear ran down George's cheek too and he felt lighter just for sharing his story with her.

"More men should be honest about their feelings. It's true, we expect our brothers and fathers to have all the answers and when they show emotion or are overcome with sadness, we go into a panic. It's not fair that we hold them to this standard too. We have to do more to support them with the little hurdles so they don't hide them from us and bottle everything up until it becomes too much." Cheryl was starting to see the complexities in the *real man* mindset.

"Yes, everyone needs to be more open and to be more human. Success is not only measured by how much money you make or your relationship status. That can't be the only way we see men as successful." George was glad he got to have this conversation with Cheryl. He didn't realize how much he needed to say these words out loud. It was therapeutic for him.

Cheryl looked him in the eyes, "Wow, you've helped me in more ways than you can imagine today. I never thought I'd have a real conversation like this at a business seminar. Things unfold in life in the most miraculous ways. I wasn't even planning on attending this seminar today. I only came here because my friend had a ticket and could bring someone for free."

George laughed, "That's the only reason I'm here too!"

They both laughed and then Cheryl said, "I guess we missed the guest speaker's presentation too! Oops."

"That means we missed the sales pitch as well!" George knew how these things worked.

They joked around about how the person at the front of the room always has something to sell before the end of the day: books, programs, retreats. They laughed about missing out on the offer and chatted until they noticed more people from the seminar make their way outside.

"It must be break time again," Cheryl suggested.

"You know what that means? Snack time." George rubbed his belly. He didn't feel the need to hide it anymore. They both got up and went back inside to treat themselves to some delicious pastries.

Ty stood at the front of the room going over his notes for the next part of the seminar. He was going to be setting up the grand finale and wanted to make some final adjustments to suit the crowd. Although he had done this many times before, he still got a little jittery just before he delivered the hook that would lead to his irresistible offer.

Everyone settled into their seats as it became time to get things going.

"Wasn't that some great info our guest speaker shared? I'm happy to see so many of you signed up for the program we are doing together." George smiled to himself. He knew there was a sales pitch. *Some people get suckered every time,* he thought to himself.

"Now that we've gone over the daily habits and the tasks, I want to talk a little bit about something that gets overlooked far too often and it will leave you feeling miserable, unfulfilled and unsatisfied once you have tasted the sweet triumph of success." George suddenly thought to himself, *How long were we outside? I don't remember hearing about setting up daily tasks?*

"One of the most important things you need to do when you are building anything in life, and I don't care if it's a business, a relationship, new hobbies, whatever it is, make sure you do this, and you have to promise me that you will. Okay?" He looked at everyone to make sure they were nodding in agreement.

"Make sure you enjoy the journey while you are focused on the destination. What that means is, you must reward yourself in various ways as you build your skills, attitudes and habits. You must reward yourself as you reach the small wins too. Don't just focus on the big wins because the big wins are far and few between. They take a long time to reach and if you don't learn to recognize the small wins you'll most likely give up before you ever reach the big ones." Ty knew this was a harsh truth but he wanted everyone to know that success is not always as rosy as it looks on social media.

"Too many great businesses fail in the first five years for a multitude of reasons but one of the main reasons they fail is because the entrepreneur forgot to enjoy the journey. Who knows someone that has worked and worked so much that they missed all the birthday parties including their own?" Ty raised his hand. Some people chuckled as he said that and then his voice softened.

"I did that. I missed my surprise fortieth birthday party because I wouldn't stop working. I scheduled meetings and wouldn't change my plans even when my brother finally told me that I needed to be there because everyone went to great effort to do this for me. Even after I knew about the surprise party and I promised to be there, I didn't show up. I went drinking with my clients and lost track of time. Can you believe that?" Ty hung his head low and wiped at his eye as he began to tell what happened next.

"When I finally got home and I went upstairs to go to bed I was so drunk I didn't even notice I was alone. I didn't notice that my kids' shoes weren't at the front door. My wife's favorite boots were gone. The house was empty and I didn't notice. That one selfish decision cost me a lot more than just money. I lost my family." Ty was ashamed of this part of his life but he knew it was important to share even if it only ever saved one kid from not having to grow up without seeing their dad every day.

He put up a slide that read:

"Life is about balance. You have to have time for work and time for play. If you don't allow these two things to co-exist, you have an imbalance." – Jay-Z

"So I want you to promise to not be like I was. Make sure you make time for the things that are important, right now. Money is only a tool. It won't make you happy. What it will do is make your life easier if you take care of the things in your life that are important to you, the things that money can't buy. So don't be like I was because once you mess up like that you'll spend a lifetime trying to make it right." Ty could hear a few sniffles in the room and knew he'd better bring the energy back up for his participants.

"I am so lucky that my family loves me more than I could imagine. They gave me a second chance and guess what I did?" Ty paused. "I put them first. I made all my decisions for them and in their best interest. I stopped taking my family and the other people I cared about for granted." The participants cheered and clapped for him.

Ty was overwhelmed by the warmth and loving energy. He felt like he had just won the championship with the love he was receiving.

"So when you focus on why you're doing your online business and why you want to be rich, remember the point is to create your best life without waiting to start enjoying your life." Ty contemplated for a moment.

"Is that a deal?" The crowd all nodded in agreement. Ty continued.

"I want to share a technique that is very important for you to start doing. It's not usually shared in a business setting but it's something every business person should be doing as part of their daily routine."

"My mentor Guru M once told me this story that I'm going to share with you now. Then I will explain it deeper afterwards, okay?"

Everyone said *okay,* almost in unison.

A Story Within a Story

A young man once dreamed of becoming a great football player. He loved the sport and felt in his heart that one day he would be great even though his skills were not of greatness yet. There were many players on the team that were far more talented.

One day he told his coach that he wanted to be great and his coach told him not every player could be great but if he gets on the right team he could be a good role player and experience being a champion with the great players on the team.

The young man was sad, as he could see that no one believed in him. No one could see what he knew in his heart would one day be true: that he had the potential and he would be great. He sat alone one summer's morning on a bench in the park, watching the birds flutter around in a playful spar. As he got lost in the beauty of the birds playing an old man came to sit beside him, a bag full of breadcrumbs for the birds in his hand.

"What brings you to the park so early in the morning, empty handed?" the old man inquired.

"I have many things on my mind and I needed to think, sir." The young man always tried to respect his elders.

The old man laughed, "Many things on your mind huh? And what could fill such a young mind?" The old man wanted to know who was sitting on his bench and why.

"Well, I have big dreams beyond the fantasies of those my age. I truly in my heart feel I will be great one day in the game of football but my coach doesn't see my true potential." He was frustrated even talking about this.

"And why do you want to be a great football player?" The old man smiled at the thought of playing football again.

"I feel it's my destiny. I feel like I was meant to be great at it and I want the glory!" The young man's voice was passionate.

"Then write down what you want and how you will feel when you reach it. Write it down on paper each night. Read it each day. Think about it before you go to bed. Make it your daily *why*," the old man shared.

The young man thanked him and did precisely as he was told. And as the football season began, one of the star players got injured and couldn't play for the rest of the year. The coach gave the young man his chance. That football season everything aligned for him and he led his team to the championship.

***

"You see there is a power in writing down what you want and how it will feel to have it. Putting it on paper somehow makes it become a must. It is like you are casting a spell that only you can choose to break." Ty watched as everyone was talking notes.

"I used this strategy to fix my marriage, to enhance my business and to create my best life. And you can use it too. Everyday."

George thought about how this would work well along with the gratitude journal he writes in each night. He started to imagine what his best life would look like and he could see how this would help him start to learn how to really think big.

The next slide was a picture of a man sitting at his computer with a look of frustration and anger painted all over his face.

George immediately felt a connection to this picture. He often felt like this when he was working on his online business. He couldn't wait to find out what this slide was all about.

Ty began to explain, "One of the most perplexing, defeating and disappointing things in the online business game, or any kind of business for that matter, is when you work so hard on your program or offer, then post it, and you get... crickets!" The participants' reactions told the relatable pain they felt.

"Nothing hurts quite like this in business. But this is one of the harsh truths we face. Sometimes people don't connect with what you are trying to offer even when you've done your research, targeted your ads, and made the offer irresistible." Ty looked into the eyes of many as he spoke.

"This will be your true test of resilience. Can you stay focused on the big life-changing goal even when others don't understand what you are trying to do or support what you are trying to do?" Ty paused for a moment to allow the participants a moment to think about the question.

George was thinking about it too. This was one of the things that discouraged him and why he often shied away from doing a lot of social media marketing. He sells using online marketing but he pays his marketing guy to do most of his Google Adwords and Facebook ads. He mainly focuses on having vendor tables at trade shows, word of mouth, and offline networking.

"This used to frustrate me and bring me to the verge of giving up. I couldn't understand how I could get it so wrong and why people weren't excited about my offer. Then one day I decided to stop worrying about it. I just decided that if the offer didn't work, I'd just make another one. I started playing around with my messaging, the style of the post, the graphics and the time of day that I was posting. I just kept adjusting and tweaking my offers."

Ty knew this was hard for people to do in a world that needs instant gratification.

"The result was traction. The more I posted the more people were exposed to what I was doing and what I had to offer and that created momentum and traction beyond what I could envision. I stopped caring about how the post did in the first hour I posted it, focusing on the quality of the post and the messaging." Ty watched as the pens were again busy.

He put up the next slide. It was an Amazon product ad.

Ty asked another, very important question, "How many of you are using the affiliate marketing model for your online business?"

Many hands went up.

"That's a great way to get started building your name and income. But how many of you have an expertise that you'd love to be able to share and build in the same way that your affiliate business works? In other words, how many of you would love to sell your own product and make 100% from it?"

This time all the hands went up.

"Well you can't." Ty smiled as many faces reflected shock.

"You need people to be able to help you promote and sell your product. And they need to get paid too. The best way to do that is to share the profit. But wouldn't you be happy giving 35% or 40% commission on a sale you wouldn't have gotten anyway?" Ty was getting to an important point about business and resilience.

Everyone nodded in agreement. George was excited to hear what Ty seemed to be cooking up.

"I started using affiliate program offers like Amazon and Clickbank to build cash flow while I modeled some of my favorite affiliate products to develop my own programs." Ty had made a lot of money doing this.

"One of the ways to keep yourself focused and motivated is to identify and offer low hanging fruit. There are many great products that you can find that will help you build your brand as a trusted ambassador of a product and at the same time introduce you to your target market as an expert. Who would love to be able to do that?"

Ty watched as the pens went down and the hands went up.

Ty pulled up another slide. This one had a picture of a tropical island resort.

"How many of you would love to have this as your office?" Ty raised his hand well over his head as did everyone in the room.

"Imagine what it would feel like to wake up in the morning with the sea breeze greeting you, the sounds of the water kissing the beach, and the warmth of the sun inviting you to jump into the cool, crisp water." Ty watched as everyone went there in their minds.

"And while you're in the water with your loved one, your phone makes a ding sound: it's a notification letting you know you just made another online sale. Imagine what that will be like for you." Ty was a master at helping his clients see their full potential.

"There's only one reason why you can't have that in your life if you want it. Only one reason. It's because you haven't decided you will. You haven't cast your spell yet in order to have it." Ty wanted to really nail this part.

"How do you think I got to where I am now? I've told you about my struggles and failures so how is it I am at the front of the room now showing you how to create a better online business?" He scanned the room before continuing.

George felt a sales pitch coming on and quickly got his defenses up.

"I have already told you how to throughout the day for those of you who were really listening. There is something that every successful person runs toward that every unsuccessful person runs away from. And at the beginning I asked each and every one of you to make a promise. Do you remember what that promise was?"

"To write down and take action on seven things today," someone yelled.

"That's right. Now as I was telling you, there is something that successful people run toward that sets them apart from unsuccessful people. All of you have already taken a step in the right direction by making that promise to take action on the things you have learned today. There is something even more influential that I've done and every other successful person has done to create true sustainable success in their life." Ty knew it was really important to build this up and nail it for it to have the maximum benefit.

George also knew what was coming and was getting ready to stand up and walk out the room but everyone was so engaged he felt trapped. He thought to himself, *I should have sat at the back of the room!*

"Successful people run toward an opportunity when they see it. They run toward the benefits whenever they come their way. They know that the right opportunity is the biggest difference between success and failure. Remember earlier when I talked about being prepared? Sometimes you have to be prepared to take action before the opportunity disappears." Ty paused for a moment and let that resonate.

"I was in a room like this, sitting where you are now, wanting to create a better life for myself but not knowing how. Guru M was speaking and he said, 'I only want those who will commit to growing and getting the most out of what I will teach them to join me. But you must not expect me to teach you, you must expect that you will make the most out of what I teach,' and at that exact moment I stood up and I joined him. You see, every successful person has someone that will guide and mentor them to reach their full potential. No one reaches success alone." Ty's assistant started handing out forms to each person.

On the form was a place to put their information and then there were a few check box options.

"I am giving you an opportunity to join my online membership mindset training for entrepreneurs. This is jam-packed with everything you'll need to really get your business going right away."

Ty pulled up a slide showing his online course graphic.

"You will get our online courses including five online business courses showing you step by step how to set up everything we've talked about today."

The slide magically added the five course graphic as Ty clicked his clicker.

"You'll also receive my five success mindset mp3s designed to show you how to create a resilient mindset and how to be prepared to take action on the opportunities that come up."

Again, the slide added this graphic too. Ty surveyed the crowd and could see everyone was engaged and eager to hear the rest of his offer.

"You also get exclusive access to our ground breaking library of instructional videos where I virtually walk you through how to set up your Facebook ads, your Messenger funnel, your sales process and so much more."

George forgot he was supposed to be on the defensive and found himself waiting to hear how much this would cost.

Ty changed the slide to a graphic showing all of the items mentioned and then as he spoke the price appeared.

"You'll get a one year membership which gives you a free ticket to our quarterly live workshop events. Now each one of these are worth thousands of dollars and I've sold these in the past for over $20,000.But I'm not asking you to make this kind of an investment today. And the reason why I don't want you to make that kind of an investment today is that it takes money to build your business and if you spend all your money buying training, you won't have any left to build and market your business. I want you to be successful so here's what I'm going to do for you."

This was the key part of Ty's sales pitch and if he did it right he would make a lot of money and help a lot of people tonight.

"I'm going to make you a special offer and I know only a few of you will take it, and that's okay. I don't want you to feel like you have to jump into this and then end up never doing anything with it. So for this offer to really work for you, here's what I'm going to do."

Ty paused as he looked at the eyes of the most engaged people. He walked from the front of the room to the back of the room.

As he began to speak, he slowly started walking backward to the front of the room again so he could keep eye contact with those whom he felt were ready to buy.

"For a limited few, I'm going to offer you one-on-one mentoring with me for a year! What do you think that would be worth to you?"

The participants excitedly wondered what the price would be.

"Let me tell you. When I got to work with my mentor it was priceless. He was able to show me how to do things in one conversation that would have taken me months to figure out on my own. Every time I spoke with him I gained so much knowledge and insight that there was no way my business could fail. This is what successful people do, they hire other successful people to teach them how to be successful." Ty knew at that moment he had the ones he needed to help on-board and ready to take action.

"Now on the page you will see different options and a blank line beside the price. So for the first package which includes the five part business course and the five mindset mp3s I want you to write $5,997. For the next package which also gives you the library of instructional videos and access to the weekly Zoom call with one of my team members for a year, I want you to write $9,447. The last package includes everything plus the one year membership which gives you a ticket to attend our quarterly live workshops right here in

Toronto, plus you can bring a family member too. It's an amazing offer and we don't usually do this but today we are offering this for only $14,999."

He watched as most of the people in the room wrote down all the prices he laid out. Ty knew what he was doing. George did too but somehow he was invested.

"Now I want you to take a pen and scratch out the prices I just told you." Ty watched as everyone in the room looked confused.

"Seriously. Scratch them out. We're not going to charge you $15,000 for this training. If you're ready and prepared to take action right now, today, this is what I want to do for you. You can pay forty percent less for each package, today only. How does that sound? Good right?"

Ty could see everyone was excited. Some were trying to calculate what forty percent of 15,000 was (6,000).

"But here's what I want to do for a select few. Remember I said you could get one-on-one mentoring with me each week for one hour? Plus, I'll give you all the other packages on the page because I really want to help you but I can only mentor a few people per year so here's what I'm going to do. I'm going to offer the first five people whose credit cards clear, the whole package for only $10,497.00. That's less than all the packages put together and you'll get all of them plus the one-on-one mentoring. And I charge $10,000 a year for one-on-one mentoring alone. But only the first five people. And the reason I do this is because I only want those of you who are really ready to get big results right now. And you know what? Seven is my favorite number so I'll accept the first seven people whose credit card clears. Paid in full. How's that sound?"

People were franticly and anxiously waiting to find out what to do next. How to be the first ones to sign up.

"So the first seven people to go to the registration table and successfully pay in full are going to get a year's worth of weekly one-on-one mentoring with me." Ty looked at everyone as he changed the slide to some testimonials of happy, successful clients he'd mentored in the past.

"You see, being prepared to pay in full pays and that's why I have learned you should always be prepared." Ty was done with his sales pitch and walked to the registration table at the front of the room.

George found himself racing to fill out his form as was everyone else. They all wanted the one-on-one mentoring. People were frantically writing and getting up to go to the table to register. Dwayne was also franticly filling out his form and they both stood up and raced to the registration table at the same time.

There was already a line twenty people deep at the registration table. George saw Cheryl there too. "They got you too huh?" she said laughing.

"Yes, but I'm not going to stand here in urgency to spend $10,000." George laughed.

"I really wanted to get the mentoring but I think I'll sign up for one of the other packages and wait for them to offer the mentoring at a discount once I'm in." Cheryl said.

"I like that strategy. Good thinking." George said. He suddenly noticed Dwayne was at the front getting registered.

"I guess my buddy is going to be way ahead of us now." George smiled.

"How did he get up there so fast?" She said.

"I guess he must have written down that he would get mentored by Ty. He made it happen." George said jokingly.

"Quick learner," Cheryl added. They both laughed as they knew this was the beginning of something more than they could see in that moment. Somehow they knew this would be a story they'd tell everyone they met, well beyond this day.

They had made an unspoken promise. A promise to always be there for each other. To honor each other and help each other succeed. This unspoken promise needed no words for their spirits had already made – the promise.

Final Thoughts

Stories at one point in time were the only way to pass on information. Throughout history the written word has been censored, forbidden or made exclusive. Even my brothers and sisters of slavery had to use stories in song to guide them to freedom by way of the Underground Railroad. Stories can be enlightening, powerful, entertaining and mind altering.

This book's intent was to do such in an entertaining, unique and profound way; as the other books in the ONE Chapter series have been designed. But this book is the second in a new turn in the series. This book follows the *Better than Fiction* technique.

These are stories both based in fiction and non-fiction concurrently. It was my intent to do this for both creative reasons and for the challenge of writing it in the way I had envisioned.

What I am sure you have discovered are many Easter eggs, as the gamers call them. I have hidden many truths within the pages of this book that apply to life in general, although this book is set in the background of a business seminar.

You can use it as a blueprint for running a seminar and I have gifted you with a great way to carry out a sales pitch at the end of your presentation. You will also find helpful ways to position the sale, create great online engagement, and create authenticity in your business. The seminar was only a setting I used to share the true message of this book. It is another not-so-hidden Easter egg.

What about the numbers in the book. Did you take time to think about why I used those numbers? Is there a message within the numbers?

For those of you in business, you can use this book as a tool to help you dive deeper into getting your business to cash flow and grow. There are many marketing and sales techniques here which I've used to grow and expand my business.

For those of you who read it for personal success and development, you will have found many super beneficial tools and methods to follow too.

For those of you that just wanted to read a great story and transcend into a world unlike the one you live in daily, I hope you enjoyed learning about the characters and the world of live seminars.

Throughout this book were many nuggets wrapped inside the insight and discovery of the characters. These stories were intended for you, the reader to use and learn from in an effort to help you in both the creation of better business experiences and more importantly in the creation of greater life experiences.

As the stories unfolded and insight gained, think of how it applies to your life and what great strides you could make if you adapted this knowledge into your daily habits and thought processes.

This is the ambition and purpose for the book. Take time to reread it slowly and pause on each nugget allowing your mind to digest it. Do not rush through it but let it linger in your mind as a gift for your future.

Thank you for investing your time into this One Chapter book. It was an absolute pleasure writing it for you. I wish you an abundance of success, happiness and prosperity.

W.T. Hamilton

"As it was, then again it will be; though the course may change sometimes, rivers always lead to the sea." – Led Zeppelin

Follow Me on Social Media

In case you didn't know, Instagram is my jam. I post behind-the-scenes footage, marketing, sales insights and motivational videos to help you build success.

I would love to have you join me on Instagram:

https://www.instagram.com/w.t.hamilton/

I am also active on Facebook, often posting more in-depth insight and hosting training sessions through my business page. Let's connect!

https://www.facebook.com/wthamiltonauthor

Get A Copy of "Your Invincible Power" motivational book series and more One Chapter Book titles here:

https://www.amazon.com/W.-T.-Hamilton/e/B00YY0S4KK

Copyright © 2020 Your Invincible Power
All rights reserved

Published by W.T. Hamilton

Who is W.T. ?

Long before he began writing One Chapter books to help driven entrepreneurs survive the entrepreneurial struggle and build success, W.T. found himself in the business world of manufacturing.

Surrounded by the opportunity of advancement and the promise of more money and company shares, he really thought he was living the dream. For a while he was. It was a wonderful dream: paid vacation time, full benefits, business trips, expense accounts, quarterly bonuses, and big titles and status.

This is what they preached at school. He even had the wife and kids. It was the complete package until...

2009. This was the game changer, this was the eye opener, and this was reality rearing its ugly head.

The great housing crash caused everything to crash including his dream life. W.T. suddenly found himself without the pretend security of having a good job with benefits. He soon realized the most risky thing you can do in life is to count on someone else to look after your income, to allow someone else to decide what your earning potential is, to leave your financial well-being in someone else's hands, and not your own!

With his eyes wide open he began to search for other ways to make money. He realized he needed to have more than one stream of income. He also knew that a nine-to-five pay cheque could help him fund his five-to-nine career and eventually he could make his five-to-nine his nine-to-five.

W.T. began this quest and started setting things into motion. The great thing about setting things into motion is that once the ball starts rolling, things beyond your imagination will appear in the form of opportunities. Some of them will be hidden and some of them not. Almost as if by design (it was by design but W.T. was not the architect), things began to fall into place in the direction of his dreams.

First, he had the opportunity to be a consultant for a company he'd had previous experience with, which needed his expertise in management and sales development.

Next, he had the opportunity to write his first book with his Mom. It was a fun and effective way to learn about the book writing industry.

As unplanned journeys go, as he started building his success, he found himself holding a microphone inspiring crowds of people from one city to the next.

Through these interactions with a variety of people and through sharing his wins and struggles as a consultant and solopreneur, he began to see there was a real need to be able to learn from real, authentic individuals.

Many were growing tired of the completely polished and put-together business guru who made millions, seemingly with very minimal struggle. W.T. knew there were those that needed to hear his voice, to learn from his unique perspective, and to learn without fancy wording or terminology.

Being the risk-taker he is, W.T. created the One Chapter Book series. Born with an optimistic mind and becoming an expert in mindset for business, he decided to incorporate these principles and concepts into his book series. He knew this would help people be able to really understand how business and life are intertwined.

Everything we do affects everything else we do. Every thought and every word paves the path for what will come next and what we are able to next achieve.

This was what drove W.T. to write these books in the way that he did. He knew this wasn't for everyone. Some will never be ready to understand life and business in this way. This is for the few who are able to open their minds to something more than living the dream. This is for those who want ultimately to live in fulfilment.

What kind of business guy thinks like this? What kind of business guy talks like this?

W.T. does. That's who he is. He is a thinker. He is a skeptic that needs to prove to himself that something works first. He is a giver, wanting to share what he has discovered so others can benefit from it too.

Most of all, he is a student always looking to grow and evolve, to expand beyond what he already knows, to see life through new eyes, and to integrate what he has learned into his daily habits and daily thinking.

It is his purpose to keep moving forward with every step he takes.

That's W.T.

Who is George?

The characters in this book have been given their names for a reason. Some are based on people W.T. knows, some are based on people that have inspired him, like Terrell Owens, Suggs, and Davis. Some, like George, are named after W.T.'s late grandfather.

None of the characters' traits or habits are based on their namesakes; the traits or habits are more related to W.T. and his experiences or has witnessed. His grandfather is a special story, however, and he wanted to honor his name and memory in the best way he knew how. So he did, through the character George.

Growing up in Canada, leaving England just before W.T. turned four meant he never got to grow up with his grandparents. When other kids would tell stories of sleepovers at their grandparents' house or going fishing with their grandfather, W.T. had none.

W.T.'s Jamaican grandfather died before he was born and his English grandfather lived too far away. He was lucky enough, however, to see him two times in his life. At least as he recalls. Sure, he'd seen him many times when he lived nearer to them but he can't remember those times.

The first and only time that W.T.'s grandfather came to Canada was the first time W.T. could then go to school and tell grandfather stories. It is a memory that W.T. cherish.

His grandfather served in the British military during World War II as part of the anti-aircraft team in charge of shooting down enemy bombers as they tried to destroy the English factories. He was barely a man at that time. He was dating W.T.'s grandmother, Emily Hall, and she would travel on the weekend from Leicester, England to the British Coast to visit him.

W.T. doesn't know much more about those times. His grandfather didn't speak much about what things he had to do to protect his country from invasion. W.T. knows it was a burden that his grandfather didn't want his four girls and one son to carry. Nor would he want his grandchildren and great grandchildren carrying that burden either. But the grandfather is the family hero. They feel blessed to have him in their family history.

The next and last time W.T. got to see his grandfather was the day before he passed away. W.T. got to spend the afternoon with him, watching black and white movies on television while his grandfather's lungs slowly filled up. W.T. was too young to know what would happen later that night.

W.T. was given the gift of having some time with his grandfather and enjoying that final last visit.

It is funny how in only eight years of W.T.'s young life, he realized that a person could have such a lasting impact. One never knows how powerful their presence can have on another and how just being there can affect them in ways one will never really know.

They will always live in the memories of the great times we shared. No one passes away from memories.

That is the story of the real George V. Hall 1917-1978, W.T.'s grandfather and the inspiration for the name of the character George.

Big Ups by W.T.

Big Up to my Mom for working and introducing me to empowerment and the power of our minds. We have created something invincible. Big thanks for your love and for always supporting me in the many adventures of life.

Big Up to my Dad for the encouragement, love and support throughout every step and also for teaching me how to be a dad.

Big Up to my kids for keeping me young at heart and always giving me reasons to laugh, feel proud!

Big up to Fanny Newport (my "ride or die") for loving me as I am and putting up with my crazy life and supporting me in not really growing up too much.

To my extended family who are always throwing love my way. Beers and barbecues for life!

To my many friends – old and new. I'm always thinking about how lucky I am to have people that come into my life for short or long term who make my life better than it would have been had I never met you. You guys and girls get a virtual high five!

And to you! Yeah you, the reader. I give you a special Big Up for investing time and money into yourself. A Big Up for the hunger to make positive change in your life, making your life the best it can be. Keep doing what you're doing. Keep reaching for the top. You got this!

Books by W.T. Hamilton

The ONE Chapter Series

a One Chapter Book
Ask For The Money

a One Chapter Book
The Million Dollar Idea

a One Chapter Book
Really Zuckerburg Really!

a One Chapter Book
The LonelyPreneur

a One Chapter Book
The LuckyPreneur

a One Chapter Book
The Harsh Truths

The Your Invincible Power Series

Your Invincible Power
Open the Door to Unlimited Health, Wealth and Joy

Your Invincible Power
How to Remove the Mental Hurdles and Limitations

Your Invincible Power
How to Tame the Ego and Fuel Your Ambition

Your Invincible Power
How to Say Goodbye to the Drama

Your Invincible Power
Incurable ?

Your Invincible Power
How to Create a Positive Relationship with Money

**The Change Book 10
Insights into Self Empowerment**

So you have done something that very few do in modern times, including myself.

You have read the entire book from start to finish. I know I made it easy because there was only one chapter to read.

But, if you're reading this too, that means you must have read the other parts of the book like the bio and the thank you sections.

Nice touch, bravo.

So this is where it ends. It's time to put what you have learned into action. It's time to make what you've learned bring you the rewards you deserve.

It's time to take action! But in the spirit of being different and daring, and because I can, I want to leave you with one last gift.

I present to you, the opening scene of this book. Thank you and enjoy!

"Reality leaves a lot to the imagination."
John Lennon

7 seconds, 7 minutes and 7 hours ago

"Why do these guys always insist on starting these things before 8 a.m.?" George didn't really want to go to this event. He was only trying to be a good friend to Dwayne.

"Come on George! These guys are all in the 4 a.m. club. Besides, they're there a lot earlier than we are my friend." Dwayne felt a little bad for dragging George out of his comfort zone so early on a Saturday morning.

"It just doesn't make sense. I mean my money is just as good at 9 a.m. as it is at 8 a.m. Hell, my money might even be better at 10 a.m.!" George was never too perky before 10 a.m.

The two friends drove down the street listening to classic rock and George's constant complaining about having to get up so early just so he could listen to an eight-hour sales pitch.

Once they parked the car and went into the hotel, George couldn't believe how many suckers got up so early just to give away their money for nothing. He really couldn't believe his eyes.

He thought to himself, *How could I get people to get up at the crack of dawn to buy what I have to sell?*

George had no idea why he was there that morning but he knew he was drawn there for some purpose.

He was about to find out that the event was scheduled at that early hour for a reason. Everything happens for a reason or more precisely because at some point in his life he asked for this exact thing.

It's often the thing that we cannot see in the moment but the thing that can only come to us if we get out of our own way and allow it to find us.

What George found was something he'd been searching for day after day and night after night, for the last seven seasons.